Modulation

MAX REGER

DOVER PUBLICATIONS, INC.
Mineola, New York

Bibliographical Note

This Dover edition, first published in 2007, is an unabridged republication of the work originally published as *On the Theory of Modulation (Beiträge zur Modulationslehre,* translated by John Bernhoff) by C. F. Kahnt Nachfolger, Leipzig, in 1904. The musical examples have been newly engraved for this edition.

Library of Congress Cataloging-in-Publication Data

Reger, Max, 1873–1916.
    [Beiträge zur Modulationslehre. English]
    Modulation / Max Reger ; translated by John Bernhoff.
       p. cm.
    ISBN-13: 978-0-486-46732-1
    ISBN-10: 0-486-45732-X
     1. Modulation (Music) I. Bernhoff, John. II. Title.

MT52.R3313 2007
781.2'58—dc22

                                   2007004094

Manufactured in the United States of America
Dover Publications, Inc., 31 East 2nd Street, Mineola, N.Y. 11501

Contents

Contents

Preliminary Remarks

This "Supplement to the theory of Modulation" is intended both for the professional musician (for those learning harmony, for pianists, organists, singers and others), and for the amateur to whom the rudiments of the theory of music are not a sealed book.

I would draw special attention to the fact that in this "Supplement to the theory of Modulation," i.e. in the examples of modulation, I have *purposely* avoided anything pertaining to enharmonics, with a view of drawing the student's special attention to musical logic; for the same reason, I have given almost all the examples of modulation by translating tonic, sub- and super-dominant into the new tonic, sub- or super-dominant, as the case may be, i.e. I have given them in so-called cadence-like form, in order to thus lay before the pupil the fundamental principle of modulation in the clearest possible manner; the analyses of the examples of modulation will at once make the fundamental principles clear to any student, even to less gifted ones! Of course, all the examples of modulation will allow of other solutions; but I doubt whether such other solutions will always be shorter—i.e. "more to the point" and more logical than those given in this "Supplement."

The musician, studying the examples of modulation with their analyses, under the guidance of an experienced teacher with a "mind open to improvement or progress," should transpose the examples into as many keys as possible, and should himself try to invent similar modulations, and even perhaps analyze his own examples of modulation in the manner of analysis adopted by me, whereby the understanding of the principles of modulation briefly developed in this "Supplement" will certainly be facilitated for him, and he will gain a considerable amount of additional insight into the subject and absolute clearness in grasping and understanding even the most complicated modulation, harmony, and counterpoint.

In conclusion, I would request that my examples of modulation be looked upon not as compositions, but that they be merely taken for what they are intended—"dry" examples explaining the simplest principles of the theory of modulation, one of the most important chapters in the whole of musical theory—especially considering the modern style of composition.

Should my little book be destined to assist in clearing up the difficulties of so manifold and varied a nature which students encounter in dealing with this special subject, the chief object of my efforts will have been attained.

Munich, October 1903

MAX REGER

Modulation

Analysis of the Examples
in Modulation

A.   From C-major to:

1) G-major   ### 2) D-major

1) G-major

Tonic C-major; use this C-major which is at the same time the sub-dominant of G-major. (Cadence!)

$$[\text{CI} \ (=\text{G}\underline{\text{IV}}), \ \text{G}\underline{\text{II}}^*), \ \text{GV}_4^6, \ \text{GV}, \ | \ \text{GI}]$$

2) D-major

Tonic C-major; relative (e-minor) to the dominant (G-major) of C-major; use this e-minor (1st inversion), which is also relative to the sub-dominant (G-major) of D-major. (Cadence!)

$$[\text{CI}, \ \text{C}\underline{\text{III}} \ (=\text{D}\underline{\text{II}}), \ \text{DV}_4^6, \ \text{DV}, \ | \ \text{DI}]$$

---

* "—"this mark under the Roman cipher means: 1st inversion (chord of the sixth),
  "="this mark under the Roman cipher means: 2nd inversion (chord of the six-four).

3) A-major   ## 4) E-major

3) A-major

Tonic C-major; relative (d-minor) to the sub-dominant (F-major) of C-major; use this d-minor, which is at the same time the minor sub-dominant of A-major. (Cadence!)

$$[\text{CI, CII} (=\text{AIV}\natural), \text{AV}^6_4, \text{AV}, | \text{AI}]$$

4) E-major

Tonic C-major; relative (a-minor) to the tonic of C-major; use this a-minor, which is at the same time the minor sub-dominant of E-major. (Cadence!)

$$[\text{CI, CVI} (=\text{EIV}\natural), \text{EV}^6_4, \text{EV}, | \text{EI}]$$

5) B-major   ### 6) F♯-major

5) B-major

Tonic C-major; relative (e-minor) to the dominant (G-major) of C-major; use this e-minor, which is also the minor sub-dominant in B-major. (Cadence!)

$$[\text{CI, CIII} (=\text{BIV♮}),\ \text{BV}_4^6,\ \text{BV},\ |\ \text{BI}]$$

6) F♯-major

Tonic C-major; dominant G-major; the 1st inversion of which is used (the chord of the sixth, b d g), which is at the same time the chord of the Neapolitan sixth*) in F♯-major. (Cadence!)

$$[\text{CI, C}\underline{\text{V}} (=\text{F♯IV}_{♮♮}^6),\ \text{F♯V}_4^6,\ \text{F♯V},\ |\ \text{F♯I}]$$

---

*By "Chord of the Neapolitan sixth," I mean the minor sub-dominant of a major or minor key, with unprepared suspension of the minor sixth before the fifth, which suspension need not necessarily be resolved upon the fifth of the minor sub-dominant. I call this chord "Neapolitan," because A. Scarlatti in Naples first treated the sub-dominant in this manner; I adopt, as the name of this chord, that which Dr. H. Riemann uses. For instance: in A-major or a-minor the cadence with the chord of the Neapolitan sixth:

NB. To obtain a smooth and faultless progression of the parts, the pupil is strongly recommended to always double the root of this chord of the sixth!

7) C♯-major   8) G♯-major

7) C♯-major

Tonic C-major; relative (e-minor) to the dominant (G-major) of C-major; use this e-minor, which is also the minor sub-dominant of B-major; dominant (F♯-major) of B-major; use this F♯-major, which is at the same time sub-dominant in C♯-major. (Cadence!)

$$[\text{CI, CIII } (= \text{BIV}\natural), \text{ BV } (= \text{C}\sharp\text{IV}), \text{ C}\sharp\text{V}, \mid \text{C}\sharp\text{I}]$$

8) G♯-major

Tonic C-major; relative (d-minor) to the sub-dominant (F-major) of C-major; dominant (A-major) of d-minor; use the 1st inversion of this A-major (the chord of the sixth, c♯ e a), which is also the chord of the Neapolitan sixth in G♯-major. (Cadence!)

$$[\text{CI, CII } (= \text{dI*}), \text{ d}\underline{\text{V}}\sharp, \, (= \text{G}\sharp\text{IV}^6_\natural), \text{ G}\sharp\text{V}^\times, \mid \text{G}\sharp\text{I}]$$

---

*Small letters always indicate the minor key, or minor triad. Capital letters always indicate the major key, or major triad.

exchanges and to receive and redeem store credit. With a receipt, a full refund in the original form of payment will be issued for new and unread books and unopened music within 30 days from any Barnes & Noble store. For merchandise purchased with a check, a store credit will be issued within the first seven days. Without an original receipt, a store credit will be issued at the lowest selling price. With a receipt, returns of new and unread books and unopened music from bn.com can be made for store credit. Textbooks after 14 days or without a receipt are not returnable. Used books are not returnable.

Valid photo ID required for all returns, (except for credit card purchases) exchanges and to receive and redeem store credit. With a receipt, a full refund in the original form of payment will be issued for new and unread books and unopened music within 30 days from any Barnes & Noble store. For merchandise purchased with a check, a store credit will be issued within the first seven days. Without an original receipt, a store credit will be issued at the lowest selling price. With a receipt, returns of new and unread books and unopened music from bn.com can be made for store credit. Textbooks after 14 days or without a receipt are not returnable. Used books are not returnable.

Valid photo ID required for all returns, (except for credit card purchases) exchanges and to receive and redeem store credit. With a receipt, a full refund in the original form of payment will be issued for new and unread books and unopened music within 30 days from any Barnes & Noble store. For merchandise purchased with a check, a store credit will be issued within the first seven days. Without an original receipt, a store credit will be issued

Barnes & Noble Bookseller
270 Buckland Hills Drive
Manchester, CT 06040
860-648-1008 06-28-07 S02167 R004

BARNES & NOBLE MEMBER   EXP:11-30-07

Modulation   6.25
9780486457321
DISCOUNT   6.95 - .70

SUB TOTAL   6.25
SALES TAX   .38
TOTAL   6.63
AMOUNT TENDERED

GIFT CARD REDEEM   6.63
Card # 6339453512887889X
AUTH CODE: #001837
BALANCE REMAINING   18.37

MEMBER SAVINGS   .70

TOTAL PAYMENT   6.63

Thank You for shopping at
Barnes & Noble Booksellers
#119789 06-28-07 01:01P JUDI

9) D♯-major

Tonic C-major; relative (d-minor) to the sub-dominant (F-major) of C-major; use this d-minor, which is at the same time sub-dominant of a-minor; dominant (E-major) of a-minor; use the 1st inversion of this E-major (the chord of the sixth, g♯ b e), which is at the same time the chord of the Neapolitan sixth in D♯-major. (Cadence!)

[CI, CII (=aIV), aV♯, aV̲♯ (=D♯IV⁶♮♮), | D♯V⁶₄, D♯Vˣ, D♯I]

10) A♯-major

Tonic C-major; relative (a-minor) to the tonic C-major; use this a-minor, which is at the same time sub-dominant in e-minor; dominant (B-major) of e-minor; use the 1st inversion of this B-major (the chord of the sixth, d♯ f♯ b), which is also the chord of the Neapolitan sixth in A♯-major. (Cadence!)

[C^I, C^{VI} (=e^{IV}), e$^V_♯$, e$\underline{V}_♯$ (=A♯$^{IV6}_{♯♮}$); A♯$^{V6}_4$, A♯$^{V×}$, A♯^{I}]

11) E♯-major

Tonic C-major; relative (e-minor) to the dominant (G-major) of C-major; use this e-minor, which is also sub-dominant in b-minor; dominant (F♯-major) of b-minor; use the 1st inversion of this F♯-major (the chord of the sixth, a♯ c♯ f♯), which is at the same time the chord of the Neapolitan sixth in E♯-major. (Cadence!)

[C^I, C^{III} (=b^{IV}), b^V♯, b$\underline{V}$♯ (=E♯$^{IV^6_{♯♯}}$), | E♯$^{V^6_4}$, E♯$^{V^×}$, E♯^{I}]

12) B♯-major

Tonic C-major; relative (e-minor) to the dominant (G-major) of C-major; use this e-minor, which is also sub-dominant in b-minor; dominant (F♯-major) of b-minor; use this F♯-major, which is at the same time the tonic of F♯-major; dominant (C♯-major) (1st inversion) of F♯-major; use this chord of the sixth (e♯ g♯ c♯), which is also the chord of the Neapolitan sixth in B♯-major. (Cadence!)

[CI, CIII (=bIV), bV♯ (=F♯I), F♯$\underline{V}$ (=B♯IV$^{6♯}_{♯♯}$) | B♯V$^6_4$, B♯V$^×$, B♯I]

13) F-major ### 14) B♭-major

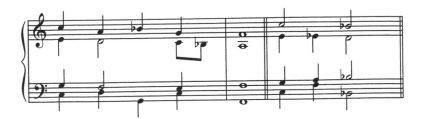

13) F-major

Tonic C-major; relative (d-minor) to the sub-dominant (F-major) of C-major; use this d-minor, which is also relative to the tonic of F-major. (Cadence!)

$$[CI, CII (=FIV), FII^7, FV \mid FI]$$

14) B♭-major

Tonic C-major; use this C-major, which is at the same time the 2nd super-dominant* of B♭-major; dominant (F-major) of B♭-major; tonic B♭-major.

$$[CI (=B♭V^V), B♭V^7, B♭I]$$

---

*The 2nd super-dominant is in major and minor keys always a major triad and generally takes the place of the sub-dominant; hence the cadence in C-major with 2nd super-dominant.

$$[CV^V = D\text{-major}, CV = G\text{-major}, CI = C\text{-major}.]$$

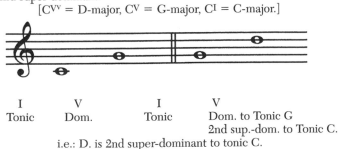

I	V	I	V
Tonic	Dom.	Tonic	Dom. to Tonic G
			2nd sup.-dom. to Tonic C.

i.e.: D. is 2nd super-dominant to tonic C.

15) E♭-major   **16) A♭-major**

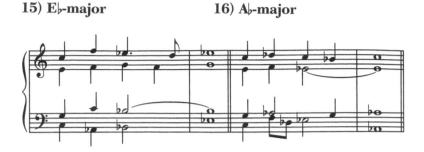

15) E♭-major

Tonic C-major; minor sub-dominant (f-minor, 1st inversion) of C-major; use this f-minor, which is also relative to the sub-dominant (A♭-major) of E♭-major. (Cadence!)

$$[\text{C}^{\text{I}},\ \text{C}\underline{\text{IV}}_{\flat},\ (=\text{E}\flat\underline{\text{II}}),\ \text{E}\flat\text{V}_4^6,\ \text{E}\flat\text{V}_3^5,\ |\ \text{E}\flat\text{I}]$$

16) A♭-major

Tonic C-major; chord of the Neapolitan sixth (f a♭ d♭) in C-major; use this chord of the sixth, which is at the same time the 1st inversion of the sub-dominant (D♭-major) of A♭-major. (Cadence!)

$$[\text{C}^{\text{I}},\ \text{C}\underline{\text{IV}}_{\flat\flat}^6,\ (=\text{A}\flat\underline{\text{IV}}),\ \text{A}\flat\text{V}_4^6,\ \text{A}\flat\text{V}_3^5,\ |\ \text{A}\flat\text{I}]$$

17) D♭-major   18) G♭-major

17) D♭-major

Tonic C-major, chord of the Neapolitan sixth (f a♭ d♭) in C-major; use this chord of the sixth (f a♭ d♭), which is also the 1st inversion of the tonic of D♭-major. (Cadence!)

$$[CI, CIV^6_{\flat\flat} (=D\flat I), D\flat IV, D\flat V, | D\flat I]$$

18) G♭-major

Tonic C-major; chord of the Neapolitan sixth (f a♭ d♭) in C-major; use this chord of the sixth (f a♭ d♭), which is at the same time the 1st inversion of the dominant (D♭-major) of G♭-major. (Cadence!)

$$[CI, CIV^6_{\flat\flat} (=G\flat V), G\flat IV, G\flat V, | G\flat I]$$

19) C♭-major   **20) F♭-major**

19) C♭-major

Tonic C-major; chord of the Neapolitan sixth (f a♭ d♭) in C-major; use this chord of the sixth (f a♭ d♭), which is at the same time, the 1st inversion of the 2nd super-dominant (D♭-major) of C♭-major; dominant (G♭-major, $^6_4$ $^5_3$) of C♭-major; tonic C♭-major.

$$[\text{CI, CIV}^6_{♭♭} \; (=\text{C♭V}\underline{\text{V}}), \; \text{C♭V}^6_4, \; \text{C♭V}^5_3, \; | \; \text{C♭I}]$$

20) F♭-major

Tonic C-major; chord of the Neapolitan sixth (f a♭ d♭) in C-major; use this chord of the sixth (f a♭ d♭), which is also the 1st inversion of the dominant (D♭-major) of g♭-minor; use this g♭-minor, which is at the same time relative to the sub-dominant (B♭♭-major) of F♭-major; dominant C♭-major; tonic F♭-major.

$$[\text{CI, CIV}^6_{♭♭} \; (=\text{g♭V}♮), \; \text{g♭I} \; (=\text{F♭II}), \; | \; \text{F♭V, F♭I}]$$

21) B♭♭-major   **22) a-minor**

21) B♭♭-major

Tonic C-major; chord of the Neapolitan sixth (f a♭ d♭) in C-major; use this chord of the sixth (f a♭ d♭), which is at the same time, the 1st inversion (chord of the sixth) of the dominant (D♭-major) of G♭-major; use this G♭-major, which is at the same time the dominant of c♭-minor; use this c♭-minor, which is also relative to the sub-dominant (E♭♭-major) of B♭♭-major; dominant $^6_4$ $^5_3$ (F♭-major) of B♭♭-major; tonic B♭♭-major.

[CI, CIV$^6_{♭♭}$ (=G♭$\underline{V}$), G♭I (=c♭V), c♭I (=B♭♭II), B♭♭V$^6_4$, B♭♭V$^5_3$, B♭♭I]

22) a-minor

Tonic C-major; relative (d-minor) to the sub-dominant (F-major) of C-major; use this d-minor, which is at the same time the sub-dominant of a-minor. (Cadence!)

[CI, CII (=aIV), aV$^6_4$, aV$^♯_♯$, | aI]

23) e-minor   24) b-minor

23) e-minor

Tonic C-major; relative (a-minor) to the tonic of C-major; use this a-minor, which is also the sub-dominant in e-minor. (Cadence!)

$$[\text{CI, CVI } (=\text{eIV}), \text{eV}^6_4, \text{eV}^\sharp_\sharp, \mid \text{eI}]$$

24) b-minor

Tonic C-major; use the 1st inversion of this C-major (the chord of the sixth, e g c), which is at the same time chord of the Neapolitan sixth in b-minor. (Cadence!)

$$[\text{CI, CI } (=\text{bIV}^6_\natural), \text{bV}^6_4, \text{bV}^\sharp_\sharp, \mid \text{bI}]$$

25) f♯-minor   26) c♯-minor

25) f♯-minor

Tonic C-major; 1st inversion of the dominant (G-major) of C-major; use this chord of the sixth (b d g), which is at the same time the Neapolitan sixth in f♯-minor. (Cadence!)

$$[C^I, C\underline{V} (=f{\sharp}IV^6\natural), f{\sharp}V^6_4, f{\sharp}V^7_{\sharp}, | f{\sharp}I]$$

26) c♯-minor

Tonic C-major; dominant (G-major) of C-major; use this G-major, which is also the sub-dominant of D-major; use this D-major (arranged as chord of the sixth), as it is at the same time the chord of the Neapolitan sixth (f♯ a d) in c♯-minor. (Cadence!)

$$[C^I, CV (=DIV), D\underline{I} (=c{\sharp}IV^6\natural), c{\sharp}V^{\sharp}_{\sharp}, | c{\sharp}I]$$

27) g♯-minor   **28) d♯-minor**

27) g♯-minor

Tonic C-major; relative (d-minor) to the sub-dominant of C-major; use this d-minor, which is also tonic in d-minor; then dominant (A-major) of d-minor; this A-major (arranged as chord of the sixth, c♯ e a) is used, as it is at the same time the chord of the Neapolitan sixth in g♯-minor. (Cadence!)

$$[C^I, C^{II} (=d^I), d\underline{V}^{\sharp} (=g\sharp^{IV^6}\natural), g\sharp^{V^{\times}}, \mid g\sharp^I]$$

28) d♯-minor

Tonic C-major; relative (a-minor) to C-major; use this a-minor, which is also tonic in a-minor; dominant (E-major) of a-minor, (as chord of the sixth), which chord of the sixth (g♯ b e) is used, as it is at the same time the chord of the Neapolitan sixth in d♯-minor. (Cadence!)

$$[C^I, C^{VI} (=a^I), a\underline{V}^{\sharp} (=d\sharp^{IV^6}\natural), d\sharp^{V^{\times}}, \mid d\sharp^I]$$

29) a♯-minor

Tonic C-major; relative (a-minor) to the tonic (C-major); use this a-minor, which is at the same time sub-dominant in e-minor; dominant (B-major) of e-minor; use the 1st inversion of this B-major (the chord of the sixth, d♯ f♯ b), which is at the same time the chord of the Neapolitan sixth in a♯-minor. (Cadence!)

[CI, CVI (=eIV), eV♯, eV♯ (=a♯IV⁶♮), a♯V⁶₄, a♯Vₓ, a♯I]

30) e♯-minor   **31) b♯-minor**

30) e♯-minor

Tonic C-major; take the 1st inversion (chord of the sixth) of this; use this chord of the sixth (e g c), which is also the chord of the Neapolitan sixth in B-major; dominant (F♯-major) of B-major; take this F♯-major in its 1st inversion, (chord of the sixth a♯ c♯ f♯), i.e. this chord of the sixth is used, as it is at the same time the chord of the Neapolitan sixth in e♯-minor. (Cadence!)

$$[\text{CI}, \text{C}\underline{\text{I}} \ (=\text{BIV}^{6}_{\natural\natural}), \ \text{B}\underline{\text{V}} \ (=\text{e}^{\sharp}\text{IV}^{6\sharp}_{3\sharp}), \ \text{e}^{\sharp}\text{V}_{\times}, \ | \ \text{e}^{\sharp}\text{I}]$$

31) b♯-minor

Tonic C-major; dominant (G-major) of C-major; this G-major arranged as chord of the sixth (b d g) is used, which is at the same time the chord of the Neapolitan sixth in F♯-major; dominant (C♯-major) of F♯-major, which C♯-major is, arranged in the 1st inversion, the chord of the sixth (e♯ g♯ c♯); use this chord of the sixth (e♯ g♯ c♯), which is at the same time the chord of the Neapolitan sixth in b♯-minor. (Cadence!)

$$[\text{CI}, \text{C}\underline{\text{V}} \ (=\text{F}^{\sharp}\text{IV}^{6}_{\natural\natural}), \ \text{F}^{\sharp}\underline{\text{V}} \ (=\text{b}^{\sharp}\text{IV}^{6\sharp}_{3\sharp}), \ \text{b}^{\sharp}\text{V}_{\times}, \ | \ \text{b}^{\sharp}\text{I}]$$

32) d-minor   33) g-minor

32) d-minor

Tonic C-major = the dominant of F-major; relative (g-minor) to the sub-dominant of F-major; use this g-minor, which is at the same time the sub-dominant in d-minor. (Cadence!)

$$[\text{CI} (=\text{FV}), \text{FII} (=\text{dIV}), \text{dV}_4^6, \text{dV}\sharp), \mid \text{dI}]$$

(Phrygian!)

C   g   A-major

33) g-minor

Tonic C-major, which is used, as it is also the chord of the Dorian* sixth in g-minor; dominant (D-major) with 7th (2nd inversion) of g-minor.

$$[\text{CI} (=\text{gIV}^3\natural), \text{g}\underline{\text{VI}}\sharp, \text{gI}]$$

---

*The Dorian sixth is the major sixth in minor, which must always be led upwards (to the leading tone); for instance, f♯ in a-minor; this f♯ can be taken as the "Third" in D-major and also as the "Fifth" in the b-minor triad! (Hence D-major and b-minor: Chords of the Dorian sixth in a-minor!)

34) c-minor   **35) f-minor**

34) c-minor

Tonic C-major; minor sub-dominant (f-minor) in C-major;
use this f-minor, which is at the same time the sub-dominant of
c-minor. (Cadence!)

$$[CI, CIV\flat \;(=cIV),\; cV^6_4,\; cV\natural),\; |\; cI]$$

35) f-minor

Tonic C-major is used, as it is also the dominant in f-minor;
then Cadence.

$$[CI \;(=fV\natural),\; fI,\; f\underline{II},\; fV\natural,\; |\; fI]$$

36) b♭-minor   37) e♭-minor

36) b♭-minor

Tonic C-major is used, which is at the same time the 2nd super-dominant in b♭-minor; dominant (f a c [e♭]) in b♭-minor.

$$[C^{I} (=b\flat V^{V}), b\flat V^{7}_{\flat}, b\flat I]$$

37) e♭-minor

Tonic C-major; minor sub-dominant (f-minor) in C-major; use this f-minor (f a♭ c), which is also the chord of the Dorian sixth in e♭-minor; dominant (B-major) of e♭-minor and tonic e♭-minor.

$$[C^{I}, C^{VI\flat} (=e\flat II^{5}_{\natural}), e\flat V^{(7)}_{\natural}, \mid e\flat I]$$

38) a♭-minor   **39) d♭-minor**

38) a♭-minor

Tonic C-major; chord of the Neapolitan sixth (f a♭ d♭) in C-major; use this chord of the sixth (f a♭ d♭), which is at the same time the Dorian sixth (D♭-major as chord of the sixth) in a♭-minor; dominant (E♭-major) and tonic of a♭-minor.

$$[CI, CVI^{6}_{♭♭} (=a♭\underline{IV}♮), a♭V♮, | a♭I]$$

39) d♭-minor

Tonic C-major; chord of the Neapolitan sixth (f a♭ d♭) in C-major, which chord of the sixth (f a♭ d♭) is used, as it is at the same time the sub-dominant at A♭-major; dominant (E♭-major) of A♭-major; tonic of A♭-major with minor seventh, which A♭-chord of the seventh (a♭ c e♭ g♭) is used, as it is also the dominant of d♭-minor.

$$[CI, CVI^{6♭}_{6♭} (=A♭\underline{IV}), A♭\underline{V}^{7}, A♭I^{7}♭, (=d♭V^{7}♭), | d♭I]$$

40) g♭-minor   41) c♭-minor

40) g♭-minor

Tonic C-major; chord of the Neapolitan sixth (f a♭ d♭) in C-major, which chord of the sixth is used, as it is at the same time the 1st inversion of the dominant D♭-major (with seventh c♭, i.e. $\frac{6}{5}$) of g♭-minor; tonic g♭-minor.

$$[\text{CI}, \text{CIV}^{6}_{\flat\flat} (=\text{g}\flat\underline{\text{V}}_{\natural}), \text{g}\flat\underline{\text{V}}^{7}_{\natural}, \mid \text{g}\flat\text{I}]$$

41) c♭-minor

Tonic C-major; chord of the Neapolitan sixth (f a♭ d♭) in C-major, which chord of the sixth is used, as it is also dominant (D♭-major with seventh c♭, i.e. $\frac{6}{5}$) of G♭-major, and this G♭-major again is used, as it is at the same time the dominant of c♭-minor; tonic c♭-minor.

$$[\text{CI}, \text{CIV}^{6}_{\flat\flat} (=\text{G}\flat\underline{\text{V}}^{(7\flat)}), \text{G}\flat\text{I} (=\text{c}\flat\underline{\text{V}}), \mid \text{c}\flat\text{I}]$$

B.   From C♯-major to:

42) E♭-major (e♭-minor)

Tonic C♯-major; chord of the Neapolitan sixth (f♯ a d) in C♯-major; use this chord of the sixth, which is at the same time the 1st inversion of D-major, the 2nd super-dominant of c-minor; dominant (G-major) of c-minor; sub-dominant (f-minor) of c-minor; use this f-minor, which is also relative to the sub-dominant (A♭-major) of E♭-major. (Cadence!)

NB. To modulate to e♭-minor, use the f-minor (f a♭ c), which is also the chord of the Dorian sixth in e♭-minor; dominant (B♭-major) of e♭-minor. (Cadence!)

$$[\text{C♯I, C♯IV}^6_{♮♮} \; (=\text{cV}\underline{\text{V}}^5_{♯♮}), \; \text{cV♮,} \begin{cases} \text{cIV} \; (= \; \text{E♭II}), \; \text{E♭V,} \; | \; \text{E♭I}] \\ \text{cIV} \; (=\text{e♭II}^5_♮), \; \text{e♭V♮,} \; | \; \text{ e♭I}] \end{cases}$$

43) A♭-major (a♭-minor)

Tonic C♯-major; chord of the Neapolitan sixth (f♯ a d) in C♯-major; use this chord of the sixth, which is at the same time the 1st inversion of D-major, the 2nd super-dominant of c-minor; dominant (G-major), tonic (c-minor) of c-minor; use this c-minor, as it is also relative to the dominant (E♭-major) of A♭-major (or a♭-minor); tonic A♭-major (or a♭-minor).

$$[\text{C}\sharp\text{I, C}\sharp\text{IV}^{6}_{\natural}\,(=\text{cVV}^{5}_{\sharp\natural}),\ \text{cV}\natural,\ \text{cI}\,(=\text{A}\flat\text{III}),\ \begin{cases} \text{A}\flat\text{V,} & \text{A}\flat\text{I]} \\ \text{a}\flat\text{V}(\natural), & \text{a}\flat\text{I]} \end{cases}$$

44) D♭-major (d♭-minor)

Tonic C♯-major; chord of the Neapolitan sixth (f♯ a d) in C♯-major; use this chord of the sixth (f♯ a d), which is at the same time 2nd super-dominant in c-minor (1st inversion of this 2nd super-dominant); dominant (G-major), tonic (c-minor) of c-minor; sub-dominant (f-minor) of c-minor, which f-minor is used, as it is also relative to the dominant (A♭-major) of D♭-major (d♭-minor); dominant (A♭-major) of D♭-major (d♭-minor); tonic D♭-major (d♭-minor).

$$[\text{C♯I, C♯IV}^6_{\natural\natural} \, (=\text{cVV}^5_{♯\natural}), \text{cV}_\natural, \text{cI}, \underline{\text{cIV}} \, (= \text{D♭}\underline{\text{III}}), \begin{cases} \text{D♭V,} \mid \text{D♭I]} \\ \text{d♭V}_\natural \mid \text{d♭I]} \end{cases}$$

45) G♭-major (g♭-minor)

Tonic C♯-major; chord of the Neapolitan sixth (f♯ a d) in C♯-major; use this chord of the sixth, which is at the same time the 2nd super-dominant (1st inversion of this 2nd super-dominant) of c-minor; dominant (G-major), sub-dominant (f-minor) of c-minor; use this f-minor, which is also relative to the dominant (A♭-major) of D♭-major; sub-dominant (G♭-major) of D♭-major; use the tonic with 7♭ (D♭-major), which is at the same time dominant in G♭-major (g♭-minor).

$$[\text{C♯I, C♯IV}^{6}_{\natural\natural} \ (=\text{cV}^{\underline{v}}_{\sharp\natural}), \ \text{cV}\natural, \ \text{cIV} \ (=\text{D♭III}),$$

$$| \ \text{D♭IV, D♭I}^{7}_{\flat} \begin{cases} (=\text{G♭V}^{7}_{\flat}), \ \text{G♭I}] \\ (=\text{g♭V}^{7}_{\natural\flat}), \ \text{g♭I}] \end{cases}$$

46) C♭-major (c♭-minor)

Tonic C♯-major; chord of the Neapolitan sixth (f♯ a d) in C♯-major; use this chord of the sixth (f♯ a d), which is at the 2nd super-dominant (1st inversion) of c-minor; sub-dominant (f-minor) of c-minor; use this f-minor, which is at the same time relative to the dominant (A♭-major) of D♭-major; sub-dominant (G♭-major) of D♭-major; use this G♭-major, which is also the dominant in C♭-major (c♭-minor).

$$[\text{C}\sharp\text{I},\ \text{C}\sharp\text{IV}^6_{\natural}\ (=\text{c}\underline{\text{V}}\text{V}^5_{\sharp\natural}),\ \text{cV},\ \text{cIV}\ (=\text{D}\flat\text{III}),\ \text{D}\flat\text{IV}, \begin{cases} (=\text{C}\flat\text{V}),\ \text{C}\flat\text{I}] \\ (=\text{c}\flat\underline{\text{V}}\natural),\ \text{c}\flat\text{I}] \end{cases}$$

NB. The modulations in Nr. 43, 44, 45, 46 to a♭-, d♭-, g♭- and c♭-minor are less recommendable, for in these, the major third of the finally reached tonic, seems more natural.

(In Nr. 42, however, the Dorian sixth c, in e♭-minor, is quite natural and also correctly used for the modulation.)

C.   From a-minor to:

47) e-minor   48) b-minor

47) e-minor

Tonic a-minor, which can be immediately used, as it is at the same time the sub-dominant of e-minor. (Cadence!)

$$[aI \ (=eIV), \ eII^7, \ eV^6_4, \ eV^{7}_{\sharp}, \ | \ eI]$$

48) b-minor

Tonic a-minor, minor-dominant e-minor, which e-minor is used, as it is also the sub-dominant of b-minor. (Cadence!)

$$[aI, \ aV_{\natural} \ (=bIV), \ bV^6_4, \ bV_{\sharp}, \ | \ bI]$$

49) f♯-minor   **50) c♯-minor**

49) f♯-minor

Tonic a-minor; 1st inversion (chord of the sixth) of the diminished triad (g♯ b d) (a<u>VII</u>); translate this chord of the sixth (b d g♯), to f♯<u>II</u> (diminished triad g♯ b d [1st inversion] [in f♯-minor] on the 2nd degree). (Cadence!)

$$[\text{a}\mathrm{I},\ \text{a}\underline{\mathrm{VII}}\ (=\text{f}\sharp\underline{\mathrm{II}}),\ \text{f}\sharp\mathrm{V}^6_4,\ \text{f}\sharp\mathrm{V}_\natural,\ |\ \text{f}\sharp\mathrm{I}]$$

50) c♯-minor

Tonic a-minor; 1st inversion (chord of the sixth) of the diminished triad (g♯ b d) (a<u>VII</u>); use this chord of the sixth, which is also f♯<u>II</u> (1st inversion!); tonic f♯-minor; use this f♯-minor, which is at the same time the sub-dominant of c♯-minor. (Cadence!)

$$[\text{a}\mathrm{I},\ \text{a}\underline{\mathrm{VII}}\ (=\text{f}\sharp\underline{\mathrm{II}}),\ \text{f}\sharp\mathrm{I}\ (=\text{c}\sharp\mathrm{IV}),\ \text{c}\sharp\mathrm{V}_\natural,\ |\ \text{c}\sharp\mathrm{I}]$$

51) g♯-minor   **52) d♯-minor**

51) g♯-minor

Tonic a-minor; translate the chord of the sixth (b d g♯) (a<u>VII</u>)
f♯<u>II</u>; dominant (C♯-major) of f♯-minor; use this C♯-major, which
is at the same time the chord of the Dorian sixth (c♯ **c♯** g♯) in g♯-
minor; dominant (D♯-major) of g♯-minor. (Notice that the
Dorian sixth must always go to the leading tone!)

$$[a\text{I, } a\underline{\text{VII}}\ (=f\sharp\underline{\text{II}}), f\sharp V_\sharp\ (=g\sharp\underline{\text{IV}}_\sharp), g\sharp V^\times, \mid g\sharp\text{I}]$$

52) d♯-minor

Tonic a-minor; dominant E-major; (1st inversion); use this
chord of the sixth (g♯ b e), which is at the same time the chord
of the Neapolitan sixth in d♯-minor. (Cadence!)

$$[a\text{I, } a\underline{V}_\sharp\ (=d\sharp\text{IV}^{6\natural}_{4\natural}), d\sharp V^6_4, d\sharp V^\times_\sharp \mid d\sharp\text{I}]$$

53) a♯-minor   54) e♯-minor

53) a♯-minor

Tonic a-minor; dominant E-major; 2nd super-dominant B-major (1st inversion); use this chord of the sixth (d♯ f♯ b), which is also the chord of the Neapolitan sixth in a♯-minor. (Cadence!)

$$[a^I, aV_\sharp, a\underline{V}_\sharp^V (=a_\sharp IV_{3\sharp}^{6\natural}), a_\sharp V_4^6, a_\sharp V^\times, | a_\sharp I]$$

54) e♯-minor

Tonic a-minor; dominant E-major; (1st inversion); use this chord of the sixth (g♯ b e), which is at the same time the chord of the Neapolitan sixth in d♯-minor; dominant (A♯-major) of d♯-minor; use this triad (a♯ $c^\times$ e♯), which is also the chord of the Dorian sixth in e♯-minor; dominant (B♯-major) of e♯-minor; the chord of the seventh (diminished) on the 7th degree in e♯-minor is used; tonic e♯-minor.

NB. The diminished chord of the seventh (in minor on the seventh degree) always takes the place of the dominant!

$$[a^I, a\underline{V}_\sharp (=d_\sharp IV_{\natural}^{6\natural}), d_\sharp IV^\times (=e_\sharp IV^\times), e_\sharp \underline{VII}^7, | e_\sharp I]$$

55) d-minor   **56) g-minor**   **57) c-minor**

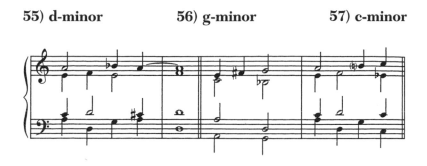

55) d-minor

Tonic a-minor; sub-dominant d-minor; use this d-minor, as the tonic in d-minor. (Cadence!)

$$[\text{a}\textrm{I}, \text{a}\textrm{IV}\ (=\text{d}\textrm{I}), \text{d}\underline{\textrm{II}}, \text{d}\textrm{V}_{\sharp}^{\sharp}, \mid \text{d}\textrm{I}]$$

56) g-minor

Tonic a-minor; use this a-minor (a c **e**), which is at the same time the chord of the Dorian sixth in g-minor; the dominant of g-minor (replaced by the 1st inversion of the diminished triad on the 7th degree in g-minor, i.e. a c f♯); tonic g-minor.

$$[\text{a}\textrm{I}\ (=\text{g}\textrm{II}^{5}_{\natural}), \text{g}\underline{\textrm{VII}}, \mid \text{g}\textrm{I}]$$

57) c-minor

Tonic a-minor; sub-dominant d-minor; use this d-minor (d f **a**), which is at the same time the chord of the **Dorian sixth** in c-minor; dominant (G-major), tonic c-minor.

$$[\text{a}\textrm{I}, \text{a}\textrm{VI}\ (=\text{c}\textrm{II}^{5}_{\natural}), \text{c}\underline{\textrm{V}}_{\natural}^{7}, \mid \text{c}\textrm{I}]$$

58) f-minor   **59) bb-minor**

58) f-minor

Tonic a-minor; chord of the Neapolitan sixth (d f bb) in a-minor; use this chord of the sixth (d f bb), which is at the same time the chord of the Dorian sixth in f-minor; dominant of f-minor (replaced by the diminished chord of the seventh on the 7th degree (e g bb db) of f-minor).

$$[a\text{I}, a\text{IV}^{6}\flat \; (=f\underline{\text{IV}}\natural), f\underline{\text{VII}}^{7}, f\text{I}]$$

59) bb-minor

Tonic a-minor; sub-dominant d-minor; relative to the tonic (C-major) of a-minor; use this C-major, which is also the 2nd super-dominant of bb-minor; dominant (F-major) (with seventh eb) of bb-minor.

$$[a\text{I}, a\text{IV}, a\text{III}^{(5\natural)} \; (=b\flat\text{V}^{\vee}_{\natural}), b\flat\text{V}^{7}\flat, \mid b\flat\text{I}]$$

60) e♭-minor   **61) a♭-minor**

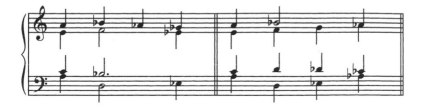

60) e♭-minor

Tonic a-minor; chord of the Neapolitan sixth (d f b♭) in a-minor; use this chord of the sixth (d f b♭), which is at the same time the 1st inversion of the dominant (B♭-major) of e♭-minor (with seventh; chord of the six-five).

$$[\text{a}\mathrm{I},\ \text{a}\mathrm{IV}^6{}_♭\ (=\text{e}♭\underline{\mathrm{V}}♮),\ \text{e}♭\underline{\mathrm{V}}^7♭,\ |\ \text{e}♭\mathrm{I}]$$

61) a♭-minor

Tonic a-minor; chord of the Neapolitan sixth (d f b♭) in a-minor; use this chord of the sixth, (d f b♭), which is at the same time the 1st inversion of the 2nd super-dominant (B♭-major) of a♭-minor; dominant (with 7♭) (E♭-major) of a♭-minor.

$$[\text{a}\mathrm{I},\ \text{a}\mathrm{IV}^6{}_♭\ (=\text{a}♭\mathrm{V}\underline{\mathrm{v}}_♮),\ \text{a}♭\underline{\mathrm{V}}^{7(♭)},\ \text{a}♭\mathrm{I}]$$

62) d♭-minor   63) g♭-minor

62) d♭-minor

Tonic a-minor; chord of the Neapolitan sixth (d f b♭) in a-minor; use this chord of the sixth (d f b♭), which is at the same time the 1st inversion of the 2nd super-dominant (B♭-major) of A♭-major; dominant (E♭-major with 7♭) of A♭-major; tonic A♭-major; use this A♭-major, which is at the same time the dominant (with 7♭) of d♭-minor.

$$[\text{aI, aIV}^{6}{}_{\flat} \ (=\text{A}\flat\text{V}\underline{\text{v}}), \ \text{A}\flat\text{V}^{7(\flat)}, \ \text{A}\flat\text{I} \ (=\text{d}\flat\text{V}^{(7\flat)}), \ | \ \text{d}\flat\text{I}]$$

63) g♭-minor

As in Nr. 62; use this A♭-major, which is at the same time the dominant of **D♭-major**; use this D♭-major (with 7♭), which is at the same time the dominant of g♭-minor.

$$[\text{aI, aIV}^{6}{}_{\flat} \ (=\text{A}\flat\text{V}\underline{\text{v}}), \ \text{A}\flat\text{V}^{(7\flat)}, \ \text{A}\flat\text{I} \ (=\text{D}\flat\text{V}^{(7\flat)}), \ | \ \text{D}\flat\text{I} \ (=\text{f}\flat\text{V}^{7\flat}), \ \text{g}\flat\text{I}]$$

64) c♭-minor

Tonic a-minor; relative (F-major) to the sub-dominant (d-minor) of a-minor; chord of the Neapolitan sixth (b♭ d♭ g♭) in F-major; use this chord of the sixth (b♭ d♭ g♭), which is at the same time the 1st inversion of the dominant (G♭-major) of c♭-minor; dominant (G♭-major with 7♭) of c♭-minor; tonic c♭-minor. (See Nr. 65.)

$$[\text{aI, a}\underline{\text{VI}}\,(=\text{FI}),\ \text{FIV}^{6}_{\flat\flat}\,(=\text{c}\flat\underline{\text{V}}_{\flat}),\ \text{c}\flat\text{V}^{7\flat}\,|\,\text{c}\flat\text{I}]$$

65) f♭-minor   66) C-major

65) f♭-minor

Tonic a-minor; relative (F-major) to the sub-dominant (d-minor) of a-minor; use this F-major as tonic. (Also in Nr. 64 at the same place); chord of the Neapolitan sixth (b♭ d♭ g♭) in F-major; use this chord of the sixth (b♭ d♭ g♭), which is at the same time the 1st inversion of the dominant (G♭-major) of C♭-major; tonic C♭-major (with 7♭♭), which C♭-major is at the same time the dominant (with 7♭♭) of f♭-minor.

$$[aI, a\underline{VI} (=FI), FIV^6_{♭♭} (=C♭V), C♭I^{(7♭♭)}, (=f♭\underset{♭}{V}^{7♭♭}), | f♭I]$$

66) C-major

Tonic a-minor; sub-dominant (d-minor); use this d-minor, which is relative to the sub-dominant (F-major) of C-major. (Cadence!)

$$[aI, aIV (=CII), CV, CI]$$

67) G-major   68) D-major

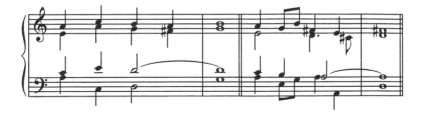

67) G-major

Tonic a-minor; use this a-minor, which is relative to the subdominant (C-major) of G-major. (Cadence!)

$$[a\text{I}, a\text{I} \, (=G\text{II}), GV^6_4, GV(\sharp), \mid G\text{I}]$$

68) D-major

Tonic a-minor; minor dominant (e-minor) of a-minor; use this e-minor, which is relative to the sub-dominant of D-major. (Cadence!)

$$[a\text{I}, aV\natural \, (=D\text{II}), DV^{6\sharp}_{4\sharp}, DV(\sharp), \mid D\text{I}]$$

69) A-major   70) E-major

69) A-major

Tonic a-minor; sub-dominant (d-minor) of a-minor; use this d-minor, which is at the same time minor sub-dominant in A-major. (Cadence!)

$$[a\mathrm{I},\ a\mathrm{IV}\ (=A\mathrm{IV}\natural),\ A\mathrm{V}^{6\natural}_{4\sharp},\ A\mathrm{V}^{5}_{\sharp},\ |\ A\mathrm{I}]$$

70) E-major

Tonic a-minor; use this a-minor, which is at the same time minor sub-dominant in E-major. (Cadence!)

$$[a\mathrm{I}\ (=E\mathrm{IV}\natural),\ E\mathrm{V}^{5\natural}_{\sharp\sharp},\ E\mathrm{I}]$$

71) B-major   72) F#-major

71) B-major

Tonic a-minor; minor dominant (e-minor) of a-minor; use this c-minor, which is at the same time minor sub-dominant of B-major. (Cadence!)

$$[aI,\ aV\natural\ (=BIV\natural),\ BV_4^6*,\ BV_3^5,\ |\ BI]$$

72) F#-major

Tonic a-minor; minor dominant (e-minor) of a-minor; use this e-minor, which is at the same time minor sub-dominant in B-major; tonic B-major; use this B-major, which is at the same time sub-dominant in F#-major. (Cadence!)

$$[aI,\ aV\natural\ (=BIV\natural),\ BI\ (=F\sharp IV),\ F\sharp V,\ |\ F\sharp I]$$

---

*Do not forget that upon the entrance of the new major-tonic, its scale is understood.

73) C♯-major   74) G♯-major

73) C♯-major

Tonic a-minor; chord of the Dorian sixth (f♯ a d) in a-minor; use this chord of the sixth (f♯ a d), which is at the same time chord of the Neapolitan sixth in C♯-major. (Cadence!)

NB. Notice the leading of the bass from f♯ to g♯! (The Dorian sixth **requires** to be led upwards!)

$$[aI, a\underline{III}\sharp\,(=C\sharp IV^6_\natural),\ C\sharp V^7,\ |\ C\sharp I]$$

74) G♯-major

Tonic a-minor; dominant E-major; use the 1st inversion of this E-major (the chord of the sixth g♯ b e), which is at the same time the chord of the Neapolitan sixth in D♯-major; dominant (A♯-major) of D♯-major; tonic D♯-major, is at the same time dominant in G♯-major.

$$[aI, a\underline{V}\sharp\,(=D\sharp IV^6_\natural),\ D\sharp V_\times,\ D\sharp I_\times\,(=G\sharp V),\ |\ G\sharp I]$$

75) D♯-major   76) A♯-major

75) D♯-major

Tonic a-minor; dominant E-major; use the 1st inversion of this E-major (chord of the sixth g♯ b e), which is at the same time the chord of the Neapolitan sixth in D♯-major; dominant (A♯-major) of D♯-major; tonic D♯-major.

$$[a\mathrm{I},\ a\underline{\mathrm{V}}\sharp\ (=\mathrm{D}\sharp\mathrm{IV}^{6}_{\natural\natural}),\ \mathrm{D}\sharp\mathrm{V}_{\times},\ \mathrm{D}\sharp\mathrm{I}_{\times}]$$

76) A♯-major

Tonic a-minor; minor dominant (e-minor) of a-minor; use this e-minor, which is at the same time the minor sub-dominant of B-major; tonic B-major; use the 1st inversion of this B-major (the chord of the sixth d♯ f♯ b), which is at the same time the chord of the Neapolitan sixth in A♯-major. (Cadence!)

$$[a\mathrm{I},\ a\mathrm{V}_{\natural}\ (=\mathrm{BIV}_{\natural}),\ \mathrm{BI}\ (=\mathrm{A}\sharp\mathrm{IV}^{6}_{\natural\natural}),\ \mathrm{A}\sharp\mathrm{V}_{\times},\ |\ \mathrm{A}\sharp\mathrm{I}]$$

77) E♯-major   **78) F-major**

77) E♯-major

Tonic a-minor; minor dominant (e-minor) of a-minor; use this e-minor, which is at the same time minor sub-dominant in B-major; use the 1st inversion of this B-major (chord of the sixth d♯ f♯ b), which is at the same time the chord of the Neapolitan sixth in A♯-major; dominant (E♯-major) of A♯-major; use this E♯-major as tonic, dominant (B♯-major) of E♯-major; tonic E♯-major.

$$[a\text{I},\ a\text{V}\natural\ (=\text{BIV}\natural),\ \text{BI}\ (=\text{A}\sharp\text{IV}^6_{\sharp\natural}),\ \text{A}\sharp\text{V}\ (=\text{E}\sharp\text{I}),\ |\ \text{E}\sharp\text{V},\ \text{E}\sharp\text{I}]$$

78) F-major

Tonic a-minor; sub-dominant (d-minor) of a-minor; use this d-minor, which is relative to F-major. (Cadence!)

$$[a\text{I},\ a\text{IV}\ (=\text{FVI}),\ \text{FII}^7,\ \text{FV},\ |\ \text{FI}]$$

79) B♭-major   80) E♭-major   81) A♭-major

79) B♭-major

Tonic a-minor; relative (F-major) to the sub-dominant (d-minor) of a-minor; use this F-major (with 7♭), which is at the same time the dominant of B♭-major.

$$[\text{aI}, \text{aVI} (=\text{B}\flat\underline{\text{V}}^{(7\flat)}), \text{B}\flat\text{I}]$$

80) E♭-major

Tonic a-minor; chord of the Neapolitan sixth (d f b♭) in a-minor; use this chord of the sixth (d f b♭), which is at the same time the 1st inversion of the dominant (B♭-major) of E♭-major.

$$[\text{aI}, \text{aVI}^{6\flat} (=\text{F}\flat\underline{\text{V}}), \text{F}\flat\text{I}]$$

81) A♭-major

Tonic a-minor; chord of the Neapolitan sixth (d f b♭) in a-minor; use this chord of the sixth (d f b♭), which is at the same time the 1st inversion of the 2nd super-dominant (B♭-major) of A♭-major; dominant (E♭-major [with 7♭]) of A♭-major; tonic A♭-major.

$$[\text{aI}, \text{aIV}^{6\flat} (=\text{A}\flat\underline{\underline{\text{V}}}\,\underline{\text{V}}), \text{A}\flat\underline{\text{V}}^{(7\flat)}, \text{A}\flat\text{I}]$$

82) D♭-major   ## 83) G♭-major

82) D♭-major

Tonic a-minor; chord of the Neapolitan sixth (d f b♭) in a-minor; use this chord of the sixth (d f b♭), which is at the same time the 1st inversion of the dominant (B♭-major) of e♭-minor; use this e♭-minor, which is relative to the sub-dominant (G♭-major) of D♭-major. (Cadence!)

$$[\text{aI, aIV}^{6♭} (=\text{e♭}\underline{\text{V}♮}), \text{e♭I} (=\text{D♭II}), \text{D♭V} \mid \text{D♭I}]$$

83) G♭-major

Tonic a-minor; chord of the Neapolitan sixth (d f b♭) in a-minor; use this chord of the sixth, which is at the same time the 1st inversion of the dominant (B♭-major) of e♭-minor; use this e♭-minor, which is relative to the tonic of G♭-major. (Cadence!)

$$[\text{aI, aIV}^{6♭} (=\text{e♭}\underline{\text{V}♮}), \text{e♭I} (=\text{G♭VI}), \text{G♭}\underline{\text{II}}, \mid \text{G♭V, G♭I}]$$

84) C♭-major   85) F♭-major

84) C♭-major

Tonic a-minor; relative (F-major) to the sub-dominant (d-minor) of a-minor; use this F-major as tonic; chord of the Neapolitan sixth (b♭ d♭ g♭) in F-major; use this chord of the sixth (b♭ d♭ g♭), which is at the same time, the 1st inversion of the dominant (G♭-major) of C♭-major; tonic C♭-major.

$$[\text{a}I, \text{a}VI \; (=FI), \; F\text{IV}^6_{♭♭} \; (=C♭\underline{V}), \; C♭I]$$

85) F♭-major

Tonic a-minor; relative (F-major) to the sub-dominant (d-minor) of a-minor; chord of the Neapolitan sixth (b♭ d♭ g♭) in F-major, taken as the tonic; use this chord of the sixth (b♭ d♭ g♭), which is at the same time 1st inversion of the 2nd super-dominant (G♭-major) of F♭-major; dominant (C♭-major); tonic F♭-major.

$$[\text{a}I, \text{a}VI \; (=FI), \; F\text{IV}^6_{♭♭} \; (=F♭V\underline{V}), \; | \; F♭V, \; F♭I]$$

D.   From C♭-major to:

86) F♯-major (f♯-minor)

Tonic C♭-major; dominant (G♭-major) of C♭-major; use the 1st inversion of this G♭-major (chord of the sixth b♭ d♭ g♭), which is at the same time chord of the Neapolitan sixth in F-major; dominant (C-major) of F-major; use the 1st inversion of this C-major, (chord of the sixth e g c), which is at the same time chord of the Neapolitan sixth in B-major; tonic B-major, which B-major is at the same time sub-dominant in F♯-major, or if modulating to f♯-minor, chord of the Dorian sixth in f♯-minor. (Cadence!)

$$[C♭I, C♭\underline{V}\ (=FIV^{6}_{♭♭}),\ F\underline{V},\ (=BIV^{6}_{♮♮}),\ BI \begin{cases} (=F♯IV)\ |\ F♯\ \underset{(VII)}{V},\ F♯I] \\ (=f♯IV_{♯})\ |\ f♯\ \underset{(VII♯)}{V♯},\ f♯I] \end{cases}$$

87) C♯-major (c♯-minor)

Tonic C♭-major; dominant (G♭-major) of C♭-major; use the 1st inversion of this G♭-major (chord of the sixth b♭ d♭ g♭), as it is at the same time chord of the Neapolitan sixth in F-major; dominant (C-major) of F-major; use the 1st inversion of this C-major, (chord of the sixth e g c), which is at the same time the chord of the Neapolitan sixth in B-major; tonic B-major, dominant (F♯-major) of B-major; use this F♯-major, which is sub-dominant in C♯-major (or chord of the Dorian sixth in c♯-minor). (Cadence!)

$$C♭I,\ C♭\underline{V}\ (=FIV^6_{♭♭}),\ F\underline{V},\ (=BIV^6_{♭♮}),\ BI,\ |\ BV \begin{cases} (=C♯IV),\ C♯V,\ C♯I] \\ (=c♯IV♯),\ c♯V♯,\ c♯I] \end{cases}$$

88) G♯-major (g♯-minor)

Tonic C♭-major; dominant (G♭-major) of C♭-major; use the 1st inversion of this G♭-major (chord of the sixth b♭ d♭ g♭), which is also the chord of the Neapolitan sixth in F-major; tonic F-major; relative (d-minor) to the tonic d-minor; use this d-minor as tonic; dominant (A-major) of d-minor; use the 1st inversion of this A-major (chord of the sixth c♯ e a), which is at the same time the chord of the Neapolitan sixth in G♯-major (g♯-minor). (Cadence!)

$$[\text{C}\flat\text{I},\ \text{C}\flat\underline{\text{V}}\ (=\text{FIV}^6_{\flat\flat}),\ \text{FI},\ \text{FVI}\ (=\text{dI}),\ \text{d}\underline{\text{V}}\sharp \begin{cases} (=\text{G}\sharp\text{IV}^6_{\natural\natural}),\ |\ \text{G}\sharp\text{V},\ \text{G}\sharp\text{I}] \\ (=\text{g}\sharp\text{IV}^6_{\natural}),\ |\ \text{g}\sharp\text{V}^\times,\ \text{g}\sharp\text{I}] \end{cases}$$

E. From d♭-minor to:

89) E-major (e-minor)

Tonic d♭-minor; dominant (A♭-major) of d♭-minor; use the 1st inversion of this A♭-major (chord of the sixth c e♭ a♭), which is at the same time the chord of the Neapolitan sixth in G-major; dominant (D-major) of G-major; use this D-major, which is relative to the minor dominant (b-minor) of E-major (e-minor); minor sub-dominant (a-minor) of E-major (e-minor). (Cadence!)

$$[\text{d}♭\text{I, d}♭\underline{\text{V}}♮ \ (=\text{GIV}^{6♭}_{3}), \ \text{GV} \left\{ \begin{array}{l} (=\text{E}♮\text{VII}), \ \text{EIV}♮, \ \text{EV}, \ | \ \text{EI}] \\ (=\text{e}♮\text{VII}), \quad \text{eIV}, \ \text{eV}♯, \ | \ \text{eI}] \end{array} \right.$$

90) B-major (b-minor)

Tonic d♭-minor; dominant (A♭-major) of d♭-minor; use the 1st inversion of this A♭-major (chord of the sixth c e♭ a♭), which is also the chord of the Neapolitan sixth in G-major; dominant (D-major) of G-major; use this D-major, which is relative to the tonic of b-minor; dominant (F♯-major) of B-major (b-minor); tonic B-major (b-minor).

$$[d♭I, \; d♭\underline{V}♮ \; (=GIV^6_{♭♭}), \; GV \begin{cases} (=bIII^5♮), \; bV♯, \; (=BV), \; BI] \\ (=bIII^5♮), \; bV♯, \qquad\qquad bI] \end{cases}$$

91) F♯-major (f♯-minor)

Tonic d♭-minor; dominant (A♭-major) of d♭-minor; use the 1st inversion of this A♭-major (chord of the sixth c e♭ a♭), which is at the same time the chord of the Neapolitan sixth in G-major; dominant (D-major) of G-major; relative (b-minor) to this D-major; use this b-minor, which is also minor sub-dominant of F♯-major (f♯-minor). (Cadence!)

$$[\text{d♭I, d♭}\underline{V}♮ \ (=\text{GIV}^{6}_{♭♭}), \text{ GV, GIII} \begin{cases} (=\text{F♯IV♮}), \ (\text{F♯V}), \ | \ \text{F♯I}] \\ (= \ \text{f♯IV}), \ (\text{f♯}\underset{\uparrow}{V♯}), \ | \ \text{f♯I}] \end{cases}$$

$$(\text{F♯VII}^{7}♮)$$

92) C♯-major (c♯-minor)

    Tonic d♭-minor; dominant (A♭-major) of d♭-minor; use the 1st inversion of this A♭-major (chord of the sixth c e♭ a♭), which is at the same time the chord of the Neapolitan sixth in G-major; dominant (D-major) of G-major; use the 1st inversion of this D-major (chord of the sixth f♯ a d), which is also the chord of the Neapolitan sixth in C♯-major (c♯-minor). (Cadence!)

$$[d♭I, \; d♭\underline{V}♮ \; (=GIV^6_{♭♭}), \; G\underline{V} \begin{cases} (=C♯IV^6_{♭♮}), \; C♯V, \; | \; C♯I] \\ (= c♯IV^6_{♭♭}), \; c♯V_♯, \; | \; c♯I] \end{cases}$$

93) G♯-major (g♯-minor)

Tonic d♭-minor, dominant (A♭-major) of d♭-minor; use the 1st inversion of this A♭-major (chord of the sixth c e♭ a♭), which is at the same time the chord of the Neapolitan sixth in G-major; dominant (D-major) of G-major; use this D-major as tonic; dominant (A-major) of D-major; use the 1st inversion of this A-major (chord of the sixth c♯ e a), which is also the chord of the Neapolitan sixth in G♯-major (g♯-minor).

$$[d♭I, d♭\underline{V}♮ (=GIV^6_{♭♭}), GV (=DI), D\underline{V} \begin{cases} (=G♯IV^{6♮}_{3♮}), & | & G♯V, G♯I] \\ (= g♯IV^6♮), & | & g♯V_♯^×, & g♯I] \end{cases}$$

94) D♯-major (d♯-minor)

Tonic d♭-minor; dominant (A♭-major) of d♭-minor; use the 1st inversion of this A♭-major (chord of the sixth c e♭ a♭), which is at the same time the chord of the Neapolitan sixth in G-major; dominant (D-major) of G-major; change the D-major into d-minor and use this d-minor, which is also sub-dominant in a-minor; dominant E-major; use the 1st inversion of this E-major (chord of the sixth g♯ b e), which is at the same time the chord of the Neapolitan sixth in D♯-major (d♯-minor). (Cadence!)

$$[\text{d♭I, d♭}\underline{V}\natural\ (=\text{GIV}^6_{\flat\flat}),\ \text{GV, (GV}\natural=\text{aIV}),\ \text{a}\underline{V}\sharp \begin{cases} (=\text{D♯IV}^6_{\sharp\natural}),\ |\ \text{D♯V, D♯I}] \\ (=\text{d♯IV}^6\natural),\ |\ \text{d♯V}^\times,\ \text{d♯I}] \end{cases}$$

F.   From a♯-minor to:

95) B♭-major (b♭-minor)

Tonic a♯-minor; chord of the Neapolitan sixth (d♯ f♯ b) in a♯-minor; use this chord of the sixth (d♯ f♯ b), which is at the same time the 1st inversion of the dominant (B-major) of e-minor; tonic e-minor; chord of the Neapolitan sixth (a c f), in e-minor; use this chord of the sixth (a c f), which is also the 1st inversion of the dominant (F-major) of B♭-major (b♭-minor).

$$[a\sharp I,\ a\sharp IV^{6}_{\natural}\ (=e\underline{V}\sharp),\ eI,\ eIV^{6}\natural,\ |\ eIV^{6}\natural, \begin{cases} (=B\flat V),\ B\flat I] \\ (=b\flat V\natural),\ b\flat I] \end{cases}$$

96) E♭-major (e♭-minor)

Tonic a♯-minor; chord of the Neapolitan sixth (d♯ f♯ b) in a♯-minor; use this chord of the sixth, which is at the same time the 1st inversion of the dominant (B-major) of e-minor; tonic e-minor; chord of the Neapolitan sixth (a c f), in e-minor; use this chord of the sixth, which is also the 1st inversion of the 2nd super-dominant (F-major) of E♭-major (e♭-minor); dominant (B♭-major) of E♭-major (e♭-minor).

$$[a♯I, a♯IV^6_{♯♮} (=e\underset{♯}{V}), eI, eIV^6♮ \begin{cases} (=E♭V\underline{V}), \mid E♭V, E♭I] \\ (= e♭V\underline{V}), \mid e♭V♮, e♭I] \end{cases}$$

97) A♭-major (a♭-minor)

Tonic a♯-minor; chord of the Neapolitan sixth (d♯ f♯ b), in a♯-minor; use this chord of the sixth (d♯ f♯ b), which is at the same time the 1st inversion of the dominant (B-major) of e-minor; tonic e-minor; chord of the Neapolitan sixth (a c f) in e-minor; use this chord of the sixth (a c f) which is at the same time the 1st inversion of the dominant (F-major) in B♭-major; tonic B♭-major; use this B♭-major, which is also 2nd super-dominant in A♭-major (a♭-minor); dominant (E♭-major); tonic A♭-major (a♭-minor).

$$[\text{a}\sharp\text{I, a}\sharp\text{IV}^{6}_{\sharp\natural} (=\text{e}\underline{\text{V}}\sharp), \text{eI, eIV}^{6}\natural (=\text{B}\flat\underline{\text{V}}), \mid \text{B}\flat\text{I} \begin{cases} (=\text{A}\flat\text{V}^{\text{V}}), \text{A}\flat\text{V, A}\flat\text{I]} \\ (= \text{a}\flat\text{V}^{\text{V}}), \text{a}\flat\text{V}\natural, \text{a}\flat\text{I]} \end{cases}$$

98) D♭-major (d♭-minor)

Tonic a♯-minor; chord of the Neapolitan sixth (d♯ f♯ b), in a♯-minor; use this chord of sixth (d♯ f♯ b), which is at the same time the 1st inversion of the dominant (B-major) of E-major; tonic E-major; minor sub-dominant (a-minor) of E-major; use this a-minor as tonic; chord of the Neapolitan sixth (d f b♭) in a-minor; use this chord of the sixth (d f b♭), as it is also the 1st inversion of the 2nd super-dominant (B♭-major) of A♭-major; dominant E♭-major; tonic A♭-major; use this A♭-major, which is also the dominant of D♭-major (d♭-minor); dominant (A♭-major [with 7♭]) of D♭-major (d♭-minor), tonic D♭-major (d♭-minor).

$$[a\sharp I,\ a\sharp IV^{6}_{\sharp\natural}\ (=E\underline{V}),\ EI,\ EIV\natural\ (=aI),\ |\ aIV^{6}\flat$$

$$(=A\flat V\underline{V}),\ A\flat V,\ A\flat I \begin{cases} (=D\flat V),\ D\flat I] \\ (=\ d\flat V\natural),\ d\flat I] \end{cases}$$

99) G♭-major (g♭-minor)

Tonic a♯-minor; chord of the Neapolitan sixth, (d♯ f♯ b) in a♭-minor; use this chord of the sixth (d♯ f♯ b), which is at the same time the 1st inversion of the dominant (B-major) of E-major; tonic E-major; use this E-major; which is also dominant in a-minor; tonic a-minor; chord of the Neapolitan sixth (d f b♭), in a-minor; use this chord of the sixth (d f b♭), which is also the 1st inversion of the 2nd super-dominant (B♭-major) of A♭-major; dominant (E♭-major) of A♭-major; use this A♭-major, which is at the same time the 2nd super-dominant in G♭-major (g♭-minor); dominant D♭-major; tonic G♭-major (d♭-minor).

$$[a\sharp I, \ a\sharp IV^6_{\sharp\natural} \ (=E\underline{V}), \ EI \ (=aV\sharp), \ aI \ | \ aIV^6\flat$$

$$(=A\flat V\underline{V}), \ A\flat V, \ A\flat I \begin{cases} (=G\flat V^V), \ G\flat V, \ | \ G\flat I] \\ (= g\flat V^V), \ g\flat V\natural, \ | \ g\flat I] \end{cases}$$

100) C♭-major (c♭-minor)

Tonic a♯-minor; chord of the Neapolitan sixth (d♯ f♯ b) in a♯-minor; use this chord of the sixth (d♯ f♯ b), which is at the same time the 1st inversion of the dominant (B-major) of E-major; tonic E-major; use this E-major, which is also dominant in a-minor; tonic a-minor; chord of the Neapolitan sixth (d f b♭) in a-minor; use this chord of the sixth (d f b♭) which is also the 1st inversion of the tonic B♭-major (in B♭-major); sub-dominant (E♭-major) of B♭-major; chord of the Neapolitan sixth (e♭ g♭ c♭) in B♭-major; use this chord of the sixth (e♭ g♭ c♭), as it is at the same time the 1st inversion of the tonic C♭-major (in C♭-major); dominant G♭-major; tonic C♭-major (c♭-minor).

$$[\text{a}\sharp\text{I, a}\sharp\text{IV}^6_{\sharp\sharp} \, (=\text{E}\underline{\text{V}}), \, \text{E}^\text{I} \, (=\text{a}\text{V}\sharp), \, \text{a}^\text{I}, \, | \, \text{a}\text{IV}^6_\flat$$

$$(=\text{B}\flat\underline{\text{I}}), \, \text{B}\flat\text{IV}, \, \text{B}\flat\text{IV}^6_{\flat\flat} \, (=\text{C}\flat\text{I}), \begin{cases} (=\text{C}\flat\text{V}), \, \text{C}\flat\text{I}] \\ (=\text{c}\flat\text{V}\flat), \, \text{c}\flat\text{I}] \end{cases}$$

A CATALOG OF SELECTED
DOVER BOOKS
IN ALL FIELDS OF INTEREST

CATALOG OF DOVER BOOKS

STICKLEY CRAFTSMAN FURNITURE CATALOGS, Gustav Stickley and L. & J. G. Stickley. Beautiful, functional furniture in two authentic catalogs from 1910. 594 illustrations, including 277 photos, show settles, rockers, armchairs, reclining chairs, bookcases, desks, tables. 183pp. 6½ x 9¼. 0-486-23838-5

AMERICAN LOCOMOTIVES IN HISTORIC PHOTOGRAPHS: 1858 to 1949, Ron Ziel (ed.). A rare collection of 126 meticulously detailed official photographs, called "builder portraits," of American locomotives that majestically chronicle the rise of steam locomotive power in America. Introduction. Detailed captions. xi+ 129pp. 9 x 12. 0-486-27393-8

AMERICA'S LIGHTHOUSES: An Illustrated History, Francis Ross Holland, Jr. Delightfully written, profusely illustrated fact-filled survey of over 200 American lighthouses since 1716. History, anecdotes, technological advances, more. 240pp. 8 x 10¾. 0-486-25576-X

TOWARDS A NEW ARCHITECTURE, Le Corbusier. Pioneering manifesto by founder of "International School." Technical and aesthetic theories, views of industry, economics, relation of form to function, "mass-production split" and much more. Profusely illustrated. 320pp. 6⅛ x 9¼. (Available in U.S. only.) 0-486-25023-7

HOW THE OTHER HALF LIVES, Jacob Riis. Famous journalistic record, exposing poverty and degradation of New York slums around 1900, by major social reformer. 100 striking and influential photographs. 233pp. 10 x 7⅞. 0-486-22012-5

FRUIT KEY AND TWIG KEY TO TREES AND SHRUBS, William M. Harlow. One of the handiest and most widely used identification aids. Fruit key covers 120 deciduous and evergreen species; twig key 160 deciduous species. Easily used. Over 300 photographs. 126pp. 5⅜ x 8½. 0-486-20511-8

COMMON BIRD SONGS, Dr. Donald J. Borror. Songs of 60 most common U.S. birds: robins, sparrows, cardinals, bluejays, finches, more–arranged in order of increasing complexity. Up to 9 variations of songs of each species.
Cassette and manual 0-486-99911-4

ORCHIDS AS HOUSE PLANTS, Rebecca Tyson Northen. Grow cattleyas and many other kinds of orchids–in a window, in a case, or under artificial light. 63 illustrations. 148pp. 5⅜ x 8½. 0-486-23261-1

MONSTER MAZES, Dave Phillips. Masterful mazes at four levels of difficulty. Avoid deadly perils and evil creatures to find magical treasures. Solutions for all 32 exciting illustrated puzzles. 48pp. 8¼ x 11. 0-486-26005-4

MOZART'S DON GIOVANNI (DOVER OPERA LIBRETTO SERIES), Wolfgang Amadeus Mozart. Introduced and translated by Ellen H. Bleiler. Standard Italian libretto, with complete English translation. Convenient and thoroughly portable–an ideal companion for reading along with a recording or the performance itself. Introduction. List of characters. Plot summary. 121pp. 5¼ x 8½. 0-486-24944-1

FRANK LLOYD WRIGHT'S DANA HOUSE, Donald Hoffmann. Pictorial essay of residential masterpiece with over 160 interior and exterior photos, plans, elevations, sketches and studies. 128pp. 9¼ x 10¾. 0-486-29120-0

THE CLARINET AND CLARINET PLAYING, David Pino. Lively, comprehensive work features suggestions about technique, musicianship, and musical interpretation, as well as guidelines for teaching, making your own reeds, and preparing for public performance. Includes an intriguing look at clarinet history. "A godsend," *The Clarinet,* Journal of the International Clarinet Society. Appendixes. 7 illus. 320pp. 5⅜ x 8½. 0-486-40270-3

HOLLYWOOD GLAMOR PORTRAITS, John Kobal (ed.). 145 photos from 1926-49. Harlow, Gable, Bogart, Bacall; 94 stars in all. Full background on photographers, technical aspects. 160pp. 8⅜ x 11¼. 0-486-23352-9

THE RAVEN AND OTHER FAVORITE POEMS, Edgar Allan Poe. Over 40 of the author's most memorable poems: "The Bells," "Ulalume," "Israfel," "To Helen," "The Conqueror Worm," "Eldorado," "Annabel Lee," many more. Alphabetic lists of titles and first lines. 64pp. 5$\frac{3}{16}$ x 8¼. 0-486-26685-0

PERSONAL MEMOIRS OF U. S. GRANT, Ulysses Simpson Grant. Intelligent, deeply moving firsthand account of Civil War campaigns, considered by many the finest military memoirs ever written. Includes letters, historic photographs, maps and more. 528pp. 6⅛ x 9¼. 0-486-28587-1

ANCIENT EGYPTIAN MATERIALS AND INDUSTRIES, A. Lucas and J. Harris. Fascinating, comprehensive, thoroughly documented text describes this ancient civilization's vast resources and the processes that incorporated them in daily life, including the use of animal products, building materials, cosmetics, perfumes and incense, fibers, glazed ware, glass and its manufacture, materials used in the mummification process, and much more. 544pp. 6⅛ x 9¼. (Available in U.S. only.) 0-486-40446-3

RUSSIAN STORIES/RUSSKIE RASSKAZY: A Dual-Language Book, edited by Gleb Struve. Twelve tales by such masters as Chekhov, Tolstoy, Dostoevsky, Pushkin, others. Excellent word-for-word English translations on facing pages, plus teaching and study aids, Russian/English vocabulary, biographical/critical introductions, more. 416pp. 5⅜ x 8½. 0-486-26244-8

PHILADELPHIA THEN AND NOW: 60 Sites Photographed in the Past and Present, Kenneth Finkel and Susan Oyama. Rare photographs of City Hall, Logan Square, Independence Hall, Betsy Ross House, other landmarks juxtaposed with contemporary views. Captures changing face of historic city. Introduction. Captions. 128pp. 8¼ x 11. 0-486-25790-8

NORTH AMERICAN INDIAN LIFE: Customs and Traditions of 23 Tribes, Elsie Clews Parsons (ed.). 27 fictionalized essays by noted anthropologists examine religion, customs, government, additional facets of life among the Winnebago, Crow, Zuni, Eskimo, other tribes. 480pp. 6⅛ x 9¼. 0-486-27377-6

TECHNICAL MANUAL AND DICTIONARY OF CLASSICAL BALLET, Gail Grant. Defines, explains, comments on steps, movements, poses and concepts. 15-page pictorial section. Basic book for student, viewer. 127pp. 5⅜ x 8½. 0-486-21843-0

THE MALE AND FEMALE FIGURE IN MOTION: 60 Classic Photographic Sequences, Eadweard Muybridge. 60 true-action photographs of men and women walking, running, climbing, bending, turning, etc., reproduced from rare 19th-century masterpiece. vi + 121pp. 9 x 12. 0-486-24745-7

PSYCHOLOGY OF MUSIC, Carl E. Seashore. Classic work discusses music as a medium from psychological viewpoint. Clear treatment of physical acoustics, auditory apparatus, sound perception, development of musical skills, nature of musical feeling, host of other topics. 88 figures. 408pp. 5⅜ x 8½. 0-486-21851-1

LIFE IN ANCIENT EGYPT, Adolf Erman. Fullest, most thorough, detailed older account with much not in more recent books, domestic life, religion, magic, medicine, commerce, much more. Many illustrations reproduce tomb paintings, carvings, hieroglyphs, etc. 597pp. 5⅜ x 8½. 0-486-22632-8

SUNDIALS, Their Theory and Construction, Albert Waugh. Far and away the best, most thorough coverage of ideas, mathematics concerned, types, construction, adjusting anywhere. Simple, nontechnical treatment allows even children to build several of these dials. Over 100 illustrations. 230pp. 5⅜ x 8½. 0-486-22947-5

THEORETICAL HYDRODYNAMICS, L. M. Milne-Thomson. Classic exposition of the mathematical theory of fluid motion, applicable to both hydrodynamics and aerodynamics. Over 600 exercises. 768pp. 6⅛ x 9¼. 0-486-68970-0

OLD-TIME VIGNETTES IN FULL COLOR, Carol Belanger Grafton (ed.). Over 390 charming, often sentimental illustrations, selected from archives of Victorian graphics–pretty women posing, children playing, food, flowers, kittens and puppies, smiling cherubs, birds and butterflies, much more. All copyright-free. 48pp. 9¼ x 12¼. 0-486-27269-9

PERSPECTIVE FOR ARTISTS, Rex Vicat Cole. Depth, perspective of sky and sea, shadows, much more, not usually covered. 391 diagrams, 81 reproductions of drawings and paintings. 279pp. 5⅜ x 8½. 0-486-22487-2

DRAWING THE LIVING FIGURE, Joseph Sheppard. Innovative approach to artistic anatomy focuses on specifics of surface anatomy, rather than muscles and bones. Over 170 drawings of live models in front, back and side views, and in widely varying poses. Accompanying diagrams. 177 illustrations. Introduction. Index. 144pp. 8⅜ x11¼. 0-486-26723-7

GOTHIC AND OLD ENGLISH ALPHABETS: 100 Complete Fonts, Dan X. Solo. Add power, elegance to posters, signs, other graphics with 100 stunning copyright-free alphabets: Blackstone, Dolbey, Germania, 97 more–including many lower-case, numerals, punctuation marks. 104pp. 8⅛ x 11. 0-486-24695-7

THE BOOK OF WOOD CARVING, Charles Marshall Sayers. Finest book for beginners discusses fundamentals and offers 34 designs. "Absolutely first rate . . . well thought out and well executed."–E. J. Tangerman. 118pp. 7¾ x 10⅝. 0-486-23654-4

ILLUSTRATED CATALOG OF CIVIL WAR MILITARY GOODS: Union Army Weapons, Insignia, Uniform Accessories, and Other Equipment, Schuyler, Hartley, and Graham. Rare, profusely illustrated 1846 catalog includes Union Army uniform and dress regulations, arms and ammunition, coats, insignia, flags, swords, rifles, etc. 226 illustrations. 160pp. 9 x 12. 0-486-24939-5

WOMEN'S FASHIONS OF THE EARLY 1900s: An Unabridged Republication of "New York Fashions, 1909," National Cloak & Suit Co. Rare catalog of mail-order fashions documents women's and children's clothing styles shortly after the turn of the century. Captions offer full descriptions, prices. Invaluable resource for fashion, costume historians. Approximately 725 illustrations. 128pp. 8⅜ x 11¼. 0-486-27276-1

LIGHT AND SHADE: A Classic Approach to Three-Dimensional Drawing, Mrs. Mary P. Merrifield. Handy reference clearly demonstrates principles of light and shade by revealing effects of common daylight, sunshine, and candle or artificial light on geometrical solids. 13 plates. 64pp. 5⅜ x 8½. 0-486-44143-1

ASTROLOGY AND ASTRONOMY: A Pictorial Archive of Signs and Symbols, Ernst and Johanna Lehner. Treasure trove of stories, lore, and myth, accompanied by more than 300 rare illustrations of planets, the Milky Way, signs of the zodiac, comets, meteors, and other astronomical phenomena. 192pp. 8⅜ x 11. 0-486-43981-X

JEWELRY MAKING: Techniques for Metal, Tim McCreight. Easy-to-follow instructions and carefully executed illustrations describe tools and techniques, use of gems and enamels, wire inlay, casting, and other topics. 72 line illustrations and diagrams. 176pp. 8¼ x 10⅞. 0-486-44043-5

MAKING BIRDHOUSES: Easy and Advanced Projects, Gladstone Califf. Easy-to-follow instructions include diagrams for everything from a one-room house for bluebirds to a forty-two-room structure for purple martins. 56 plates; 4 figures. 80pp. 8¾ x 6⅜. 0-486-44183-0

LITTLE BOOK OF LOG CABINS: How to Build and Furnish Them, William S. Wicks. Handy how-to manual, with instructions and illustrations for building cabins in the Adirondack style, fireplaces, stairways, furniture, beamed ceilings, and more. 102 line drawings. 96pp. 8¾ x 6⅜. 0-486-44259-4

THE SEASONS OF AMERICA PAST, Eric Sloane. From "sugaring time" and strawberry picking to Indian summer and fall harvest, a whole year's activities described in charming prose and enhanced with 79 of the author's own illustrations. 160pp. 8¼ x 11. 0-486-44220-9

THE METROPOLIS OF TOMORROW, Hugh Ferriss. Generous, prophetic vision of the metropolis of the future, as perceived in 1929. Powerful illustrations of towering structures, wide avenues, and rooftop parks–all features in many of today's modern cities. 59 illustrations. 144pp. 8¼ x 11. 0-486-43727-2

THE PATH TO ROME, Hilaire Belloc. This 1902 memoir abounds in lively vignettes from a vanished time, recounting a pilgrimage on foot across the Alps and Apennines in order to "see all Europe which the Christian Faith has saved." 77 of the author's original line drawings complement his sparkling prose. 272pp. 5⅜ x 8½. 0-486-44001-X

THE HISTORY OF RASSELAS: Prince of Abissinia, Samuel Johnson. Distinguished English writer attacks eighteenth-century optimism and man's unrealistic estimates of what life has to offer. 112pp. 5⅜ x 8½. 0-486-44094-X

A VOYAGE TO ARCTURUS, David Lindsay. A brilliant flight of pure fancy, where wild creatures crowd the fantastic landscape and demented torturers dominate victims with their bizarre mental powers. 272pp. 5⅜ x 8½. 0-486-44198-9

Paperbound unless otherwise indicated. Available at your book dealer, online at **www.doverpublications.com**, or by writing to Dept. GI, Dover Publications, Inc., 31 East 2nd Street, Mineola, NY 11501. For current price information or for free catalogs (please indicate field of interest), write to Dover Publications or log on to **www.doverpublications.com** and see every Dover book in print. Dover publishes more than 500 books each year on science, elementary and advanced mathematics, biology, music, art, literary history, social sciences, and other areas.